Lo

by
Kendall D. Glaspie

Loved-Unloved by Kendall Glaspie

Published by Kendall Glaspie

Copyright © 2022 Kendall Glaspie

For permissions contact: glaspietheartist@gmail.com

Cover by Kendall Glaspie

ISBN: 9798794885330
Imprint: Independently Published

Printed in United States

1st Edition

Table of Contents

Chapter 4

Chapter 5

Author Biography

Kendall D. Glaspie is a Harlem based African-American author and poet. Born July 3, 1980, he grew up in Spanish Harlem. His passion for writing developed out of a desire to connect people through performing arts. Kendall's literary expression is self taught. His body of work explores intersections between culture, economics, environment, politics, and race.

Preface

This poetry book, Loved-Unloved was born out of the desire to find purpose in love. For the larger part of my life, a purpose-filled life and love have been diverging narratives tearing at my manhood. It has taken me many hours to mine thoughts and find the embers that still ignite my pain. I am a collection of sacrifices, an overdraft of choices, and a prisoner to my consciousness. I am still arriving.

This book is about the grace afforded to me on my journey to become whole within a society for which half the people wish me to be broken. This book is a culmination of four decades of being black in America, three hundred thousand and four hundred hours of living in the shadows of oppression, and the accumulation of two Lake Tahoe's of tears squeezed into four thousand words. My quest for wholeness is not mine alone. Accuracy for this topic requires your reflection. Why do you love me? Why do you hate me? Why are you impartial? This book is about asking myself those critical questions and an invitation to help me and others discard antiquated constructs that no longer serve this day.

This book is evidence that my faith is stronger than circumstance. It's a testament that trauma can become a triumph. It's the revelation that my truth can coexist with yours. That our words have meaning beyond their intent. That I am Loved-Unloved and a master of puzzles.

Introduction

Loved-Unloved is a collection of poems that explore complex dynamics that influence the identity and psyche of black men in North America. It investigates what the construct of love means to us as individuals and as a collective. It excavates multiple reflections and feelings at various inflection points throughout my life as well as others.

Each chapter curates writing based on specific developmental stages that significantly shape our paradigms and some daggers beneath the trauma. The journey is not static. Instead, lessons are extracted and detracted from our experiences across disciplines, relationships, and society. Embrace the ebbs and flows I share as your own.

I pray that you meet a new you along the journey and we are able to contribute further to the discussion of identity together.

Chapter 1

"A child is at the mercy of cardiologist that refuse
residency,
some just know the way"

KG

Sweet Spontaneity

With the might of the mind
two vessels frolic
disarmed bare-skinned
tryst of aerosol arousal
fusion of cologne and perfume

the real learning begins
a trimester
auscultate voices
through bone and flesh
I've outgrown this lagoon

light hails the first breath together
the swift of a finger
scooped!
a majestic presence

layers of warmth and complex feelings
skin to skin with my host
assigned to nourish thy spirit
a spoon carved just for me

Grand-Child

Curiosity contained to an Harlem apartment
the vantage-point 19 stories above
high enough to see the stadiums gleamer
Shea and Yankee
low enough to see reality
distance that could only speak through movement
a windowsill

What could be touched?
the trinkets on grandma's wall unit
small enough to handle in imagination
a porcelain maid's bell
the hollow with wire and ball
sounds pitched high when I rang
my ears found no pleasure but I rang on
"Stop!" Grandma yelled to protect her toys
a playground

"I'm sorry Ma-Ma. I'm bored."
"What are you doing?" I ask
her eyes are glued to the Soaps
the show's score drums up tension
"Why is she yelling at him Ma-Ma?"
her arm, half olive branched
towards my mouth
a guardian

Our meeting of words
pushed to a commercial break
"What do you want for dinner Grandchild?"
fried chicken would often be my reply

an inquiry of shoestring french fries
earn me a trip to the deep freezer
on top rest bread, wheat and white
I return to report my findings
hooray, there's enough to feed several
and ice-cream
a hunger

keys jiggle briefly with a ritualistic precision
not a fumbling but a calculated flick
a gentle giant enters baring gifts
a family sized meal
my preferences factored into the order
"Grandpa!"
I used the label and dad interchangeably
Kentucky Fried C
it was still chicken
a red and white lunch box
with a stench of the blues
to complete the emblem
a flag

we are American
these are my heroes
indebted to their sacrifices
a prison to their silence
reflections of their pain
unspoken regrets of time slipping away
birthing seven, burying four
five hearts remain
they've had lots of practice
a home

my quiet place
home-base and traditions
the grandest place available
a small world
big love
tiny
me

Babysitters

Fred was a bedrock
Wilma gave Pebbles and I the same vitamins
Betty loved purely, Barney loved simply

Daphne was mysteriously cute
Scooby was innocently a mess
Shaggy must of been half-baked

Charlie was my age
Snoopy the same color as the rest
Franklin was brown but had no last name
we were probably family

Bugs showed me how to eat veggies
side chewing with molars
carotene and calcium strengthen my eyes
to see he manipulated trauma

I knew Yogi before I knew meditations
eastern medicines were south-parked
The modern family next door was the Jetsons

Mostly the same complexion as the teachers that fled my
community after 3

Mickey became Mighty
Jerry couldn't keep up with Speedy
Fievel dodged Danger to make it to an America near you
where most mice had bonds out for their life

"Knowing was half the battle"

"The power is yours"
"Everything was important. Either that or nothing was."

McDuck was about his purse
Winnie gorged food that wouldn't spoil
Bartholomew chased cracks in societal boundaries
The Dark Knight showed who was worth saving
He-Man was the master of the universe
Optimus showed it was possible to change…

Moods with the flick of a channel
they talked, I listened
they taught, I studied
What it means not to see your reflection
too bad I can't call to catch up
no fret
I bet they don't even remember

Frying Pan

Encrusted lava rocked sides
shined brilliance from lard and corn oil
reaching every crevice
heavy, solid
it stood out in the cabinet
a fixture to the stove
the meals that came from you
Cast and Iron
if only you could tell stories

No Hot Sauce Please

Before I could speak
before being weaned from the bosom
sustenance betrayed me just as adults
a young aunt rambunctious in her care
not even a warning

I recall beads of sweat culminating on my forehead
pain in my scrunched up face surely conveying disdain
memory, I observe like a fly on the wall
the panicked off-beat dancing of a toddler
skirmishing to rid the fire from underneath his tongue

I recall no water
my nose is the guide on this journey
the teleporting power of smell
soured sweet pollened barbecue
I pessimistically sit down to fine dine

Interrogating the menu screening for spiced and pickled
"I have allergies to vinegar, please notify the chef"
the waiter replies with an "absolutely sir"
I can see through his pondering eyes
he's a lover of sauces
an untainted palate

he understands nuances of taste and smell, an artist
I understand nuances of cause and effect, a muse
we speak different languages
he will need a reminder for all that is normalized
today, drinking alone will earn me this seat
I'll have anything but a Bloody Mary

"something strong,
something clean,
and on the rocks"

History of Love

B, L, A, C, K
BLACK
a social construct aimed at robbing you of your history

HISTORY
a record
a study of origins, events, and collective choices that
influence society
today

Your HISTORY
began way before the American Dream made declarations
to be your nightmare
before your pigment became the scorn of this world

grandma's, daddy, mother's, father's father, mom's, pop's
lineage
made in his perfect image

they were men
they were women
perfectly imperfect human beings
fully encompassing the good and bad we all have
regardless of race, creed, or religion

HISTORY
I caution you not to cloak, quote, unquote "Black History"
in the experiences of icons we so readily summon as
examples of exemplary blackness

close your eyes with me

breathe
breathe deeply for history is the moment you stand in,
knee-deep

we can see further through our tears than the lens of a
telescope
we can walk further with a hymn on our heart than with
hate on our shoulders
we have and we can do anything with love

if you want to honor our history think about who taught
you to LOVE

Who fed you?
Who clothed you?
Who bathed you?
Who wiped your tears?

Who said it?
Who meant it?
Who lived it?
Who gave it without expectations?

Who did not subscribe to the narrative of you being less
than?

smell it
home cooked meals feeding more than your belly
see it
smiles warming your spirit with tenderness and a sense of
belonging

feel it

a hug embracing and protecting you from this world
the resilience of your brilliance is heaven sent

the words that have proceeded this moment are but a
memory
yesterday is a horizon, yet you keep rising
a living, breathing, history
you are!

with the stories on your heart, you are Black History
with the swagger in your being, you are Black History
with the grit in your purpose, you are Black History

so I'll ask and you'll decide
Who? WHO?
Who will you teach to LOVE?
Who will you teach Black History?

Chapter 2

"Measure my weight through the words that I have spoken
and their roots that hold me to the scale"

KG

I am

The glue to the universe
a blanket for the stars
the rest behind eyelids
the moment you switch off
primary and neutral
oil in a well
the feet to your cars
what remains behind fires
the uniform for formal
secret service en route
ink choice for legal
placemats to the road
cavities to your oven
braces to the stove
an albino to a snow leopard
a crow and a bat
Clayton to Langston
Ray and his prism
I am foreverness

My Nigga

Jovial renditions
accented Spanglish and Arabic
"my nigga"
injected with the casualness of a "hello"

dog ears pointed like antennas
that word means many things to me
I lose words to the distance
my eyes distract me
I've never seen her before
a beautiful a woman

"nigga stop playing"
their tone registers as private banter
they notice her too
she's made it into their fantasies
a voice sweetened with intent
"would you like a bag ma'am"
aware of conditional politeness

I return to my search
bypassing the chips that use to be a quarter
landing on cashews packaged blue and tan
"...this fucking nigga...
he doesn't know if he wants to be black or white."
Daily News headline sparks debate
I approach with money in hand
"Hey brother,..."

I am countered with
"What's good my nigga?"

I massage the fold of my brows
plotting my next words
surveying candy in jewelry cabinets
is this the same as he who thinks I should be a slave?
"a loosie and a Snickers bar" I reply
tobacco and sugar to subdue my desire
I'm addicted
I guess I'm just a different type of nigga

Philophobia

Orphaned, I recall often
longing for belonging
apparent
"these are not your parents"
tread lightly
politely

I am tolerated by liberated livers
fortunate givers
of bread
I could be dead
surprise intervention of my demise

forget love
I have other drugs
drug through sane veins
of muscular vascular cardio
sowing seeds of owing

myself for every spare berry
loaned to calories prone
to burnt ratios of stoned kidneys
perishables feeding fragility through utility

on the basis of chasing basics
I want not to want
more than assured shores
ordered water draining through

new creeks with contained leaks
drifting aloft soft winds

I pretend it is possible to mend
brokenness within

smile away wild child
conducting grown folk business
fizzing
under coats coating displaced
feelings dealing blows low

endorphins trapped intact
with feelings unfelt
beyond rungs on Maslow's slow
ascent to self actual factual

loving me escapes me
so I sit out, open to subbing for a sub for now
a patient to patience
when IT surfaces I surrender to evasiveness
a feeling yearned too firm

underdeveloped throttled bottles
never filled nor willed
I want what haunts me so I flee
or stay longer than I should

corroding before exploding
unions wedding platonic monuments
past-tense, forgotten rotten
I'm a stoic heroic

partnering with seclusion solutions
abusing none disillusioned
with hopes of penetrating my waiting

to fall away with minimum collateral damage

from bronzed baby shoes boozed
with hollow tips, snipped
by still born thorns in my Achilles
armored dilemma

four seasons of winter
cold to colder
reassured by all that board my harbor
for a pit stop

I Belong to No One

At work I make sure
my ideas stand as bold
as my hair

weaved tightly
and made for the sun
wool contemplation

there is hesitation
to disclose my heart
closely distant

I collaborate out of
necessity
these are not friends

allies for a W-2
thirty off the top

so I hide quarters
within safe quarters

who knows Me
as I know them?
I've listened

to chattered whispers
beyond the naked ear

I hear
through tone allegiances under skin

I smile for cover

I'm nothing
but an idea
affirmative flare

I'll be the first to deliver
and the first
to be sacrificed

martyr here Mr. H R

I belong to no one

in her I am
lost In memories to come
I see past forward

wounds patched closed
seeds in her hands
badges of scabs

I'm prepared
to change gauzes
sculpting to precious

decisions about us
at arm's length
I've wanted to offer advice

gentle suggestions from
shared sacred words
I received

blank responses await
I'm illiterate
to the suppression of secretes

so I drain
expectations
strained through wickeder meshed tops

there are spills
and splatters
beneath my feet

hooked by
"I love you"
but it's not working

so I concur
and add space between
for her
for me
for better

free as a bird

I belong to no one

at the ballot
I wait for power
to exchange hands

with the pace
of this line

hope dissipates
with the news

cycles churning backwards
roles reverse
current, currents

standing still
politics defying
wisdom of logic
for the greater good

grained opioid salt
on a scale
of concrete
demolished
by veto

blind loyalty
to the louder voice

echoing within chambers
immune to
my class-ship
not the captain

more like an oar
a tool to push
forward those on board
this feels of chore

count my vote
forget my face

I'm an address
unaddressed
and unimpressed

I belong to no one

brother from afar
I admire your threads
not sold here

imported
from a land far away
televised still as a jungle
projections of bad writers
fill me in

What have I missed?
400 years
eclipsed

surely there's
commonalities
shades on the same diaspora
away, we stray
on streets of this Mecca
half enlightened
fragmented stories

my curiosity permeates
from our differences
dress me in culture
let us connect flags of our beating hearts
fill gaps

weave colorful blankets together
be family again

I belong to no one

The Walls We Make

Walls can be broken
with open hearts
and a moment

I'm ready to make a leap
Wings are spread
sails are open
Is it now?

ready to migrate towards the equator
invested in bliss
the World is small
I need no more fences
no more bridges

I must fly

Chapter 3

"My contribution begins with awareness,
it stops when I can't take my own advice"

KG

My Walking Tour

You're a bit late for the Puerto Rican Day Festival
too soon for Grants Tomb
anywhere you survey, the Renaissance still lives

This is the precipice of the exonerated Five
110th Street and 5th
the marathon runs right through
that boathouse came later
and the lake tells stories
book covers of algae
I've stood in its center
hollowed and forgotten
bodies were fished out

Miles used to live on the other side of this park
on his birthday many come to gather
music in the streets, horns and drums,
hustle and bustle, rhythm in our feet

"This way, please!"
off we go to Madison
El Barrio, Spanish fly
borders drawn where the metro north
decides to consider it's neighbors
noise variances observed
below 97th,
above, it screeches loudly up past 125th
where precursors for gentrification have circumcised parts
of the community
everything's still fragile, new skin is raw

This is where a neighbor DJ got gunned down in front of a
squadron
police became onlookers
Believe it or not
the purp got away

this used to be a crackhouse
and dope was sold over there
that used to be a number hole,
it had everything but lotto
mobsters congregated next door

A few blocks up, Hector Camacho spared with Lucian
iron Mike visited that basement
and heroes arrived to a cheer
people stopped fighting
guns were kept near

that used to be affordable until a few politicians auctioned
it off
that use to be Mark something … an artisan mall
vacant for the last few decades, what will become of it?

oh that's Columbia's,
you know…bittersweet in its glory
not one neighbor I know graduated there
so close, but so far

that's the Cotton Club
you know we still can't get in?
but just over there
the Apollo still thrives

that's the States building
Clinton opened its gates
that's the same bank for when landlords raise rent
they raised their rates

there's a magic trio
McDonalds, Spirits, and Churches
staples in the community
importance not in that order

Those are called projects
forever in development
they've invested in the bricks
but forgot about the people
that's my favorite eatery
calories are off the chart
literally not listed

This is my part of Harlem
This is my heart

Road Kill

My spirit was left aside a road
miles ago an enemy stole
all I refused to claim in glory

wings made of sowing parables
and robes cloaked in maternal grace
God sent an Angel in you

to heal through instruction
to carry hope and reconstruct
heavenly purpose lived through

what a gift you are in our God
restore, heal, lead
keep doing what Angels do

Plunge

The unexplained
manifested once more
a diving board
became a catapult

faith guided
me to the edge
of existence
potential, energy,
intentional,
risks of vulnerability

I can't swim nor fly
my strength
is that of a mere being
master of my environment
I can erect ladders
from the seas floor

but I'm not sure I can
ascend to the surface
my breath has already been taken away

Uproot Racism - Tribute to Trayvon Martin

At the root, conflict is the clash of ideas
but what happens when littered terrain only allows for the
gardener to manicure the branches too fragile to support a
noose?

purposeless DEAD weight. Why wait?...
to pour acid on that which brings forth rotten fruit
oh tree of life...why does vengeance appear to belong to the
hate Zimmered men?...

racing to uphold a justice without just... is ice... cold
why has my brother from another been taken by the
manifestation of a sickened-idea?
the idea that brown skin and coarse hair is the spoil of the
world...
that he, that we...are inferior to the possessors of the forged
deed to this land for which we stand
that interrupted histories are sub par to a legacy of barbaric
acts premised on greed and corrupted hearts

an idea…
an idea, please contend or counter...or forever hold your
breath
spare me the politicized propaganda or footage of Lipton
Tea'er demanding proof of belonging
an idea that the monumental elections of the 44th and 45th
president of the U S of A, could challenge the new Jim
Crow and the Uncle Ruckus of the Supreme court
that fear and hate have been uncontested unifier's to the
pledge of allegiance, under racism, indivisible by

legislation that continues to press... my...patience

How can accomplished scholars not see the correlation
between affirmative action and the miseducation of the
oppressed; generational displacement?
Clue klutz Judge, please enlighten me on how tainted
perception could take precedent over irrefutable fact

If Trayvon was white, there would not have been suspicion,
there wouldn't have been the pursuit of prosecution without
due process, nor a dislodged pistol, ...
or a precious life cut short
I submit that this unkempt forage of land is contaminated
by poisoned ivory and genetically modified herbicide
aimed at "he" as an idea...
"me"as an idea
I beg of you to show me that there is a way to uproot
inequalities centered on hate without igniting an all
consuming melting pot
tell me the Martin family will see justice
tell me we are closer to muting this disease of the mind
tell me an uprooting is near
or forever hold your breath

A Walk Without the Shepherd

We walked side by side
on a paved path with cracks in the asphalt
barefooted
present to the ground beneath
eyes fixed on the next steps
jagged rocks and edges

in each other's peripheral
we posture to appear unaffected
strong, we know how to walk alone
we've strolled with others
but this terrain is unforgiving

each planting of feet more excruciating
a reminder of missteps along our journey
our souls must try to be whole
maybe we walk alone and light the each other's way
we should be able

but legs are weak
hearts are exhausted
I don't want to leave your side
but this is a must
can we crawl tomorrow to build confidence?
endurance?
I'll trail for a minute or move ahead if trusted

keep my voice near
stable your strut
sprinting laying down
this progression is slow

I've reached as far as I can extend
I know God's arms are longer

Prescribe

Prescribe me an account with no overdrafts
surpluses of sacrifices before me
a mansion on the hills
big enough to house generations
a garden to pick meals
physicians that treat me whole
bedside manners of a saint
a mind to see through hurt
a heart to forgive with grace
an opportunity to navigate way less barriers
ballet feet to pivot to this song
more years to raise up a child
prescribe me anything but a pill
prescribe me what is just

Chapter 4

"Thinking protects feeling,
feeling protects thinking,
prayer protects both"

KG

Life hacks

When short on gas
shift to neutral on downhills

If out of sugar
find the sweetness in the water

When the sun doesn't shine in
paint walls bright colors

If your credit has taken a hit
don't attempt to renegotiate just yet

Pray through it all

When school isn't worth the cost
curate lessons on YouTube

If you lie about your character
follow up with the work to be better

when your only counsel is you
try therapy

If your heat turns off
make it an indoor camping trip

Pray through it all

when someone you love dies
celebrate their life

If someone you detest dies
celebrate their life

When it's too big of a pill to swallow
take smaller doses

If cheese gives you bubble guts
indulge in private

Pray through it all

When someone looks at you to see their reflection
smile at the mirror

If there's a leak on the roof
wait for it to dry before you patch it

When the elevator doesn't work
make friends with neighbors on lower floors

If today looks crappy
and tomorrow looks worst

Pray through it all

Miming for Healing

Tears fell in rapid succession from her eyes that morning
she struggled to achieve mental clarity
thoughts bouncing erratically
with each beat
with each percussion radiating from the left side of her
chest
cavity

there it was…. demons of the past and angels of the present
complex dimensions aligned in one scope
depth to field
depth to focus
the SUBJECT
a developmentally challenged being
 in an unforgiving world
refusing to acknowledge the past
… reality!

her heaven on earth gone
innocence sucked dry
thief!…childhood stolen in the mist of night
thief! robbed of self
too long she stood afloat
by holding on to a euphoric purpose
an endless source
of an array of emotions that lay dormant

love was a fear that matured to hate
it had become an oxymoron
a played out contradiction
a ploy concocted by the enemy of her soul

at that hour, that place

she found herself on a mental and spiritual hot-seat
the need to reflect
to justify and compartmentalize
the rationale of the now
"do I attribute this to conditioning of circumstance"
neglect of divine guidance
or the multitude of her own inadequacies'
or a prism of doublethink, perhaps all of the above?
she had been operating on a spiritual deficit so long
that she now longed for misery?
the familiar?

wired like those that failed miserably to assimilate to the
certainty of
adversity?
she forced herself to walk with without seeing
a pace slow and steady

the alter
ah, there it was
tear ducts aroused, ready to flow free
fixated to discern causation for the uneasiness of her soul
instances of reactions short fused and cold
she arrived on a train called mercy

able to finally make out the abstract image that originated
in that reoccurring dream
and manifested in this world
for the first time in her life
she cried for joy
not deceit, pain or agony... but joy

the past had passed
the well had dried
soil tilled ripe

Antiquated Love Advice

"Conventional time" only accounts for the
moons we've yet to sit under
the earthshine we've yet to toast to
the journeys we yet to take
but the essence of your heart is timeless
so I count not the hours nor the days but
the moments time stands still when we
stare in each other's eyes

"Conventional wisdom" only accounts for yesterday's
lessons
that have stumbled forward to the footsteps of today
so I accept the linger of past possibilities
for they are now renewed in a release to the winds
what stays shall be nurtured to health
what leaves I send whispers guiding them to land gently on
the heart that needs a lesson
I inhale to make space for all of you with the expectation of
nothing for now

"Conventional" is a Box for which we can't belong
so I beat back the arrogance of group-think shaped by fear
shaped by unfulfilled vessels navigating the wilderness of
within
yet they seek outward one after another
so from here on out when the analog arms stretch towards
the eleventh hour
and eleven minutes accrue
I'll make my "conventional" wish for you

Redacted

_____

because I am hurt

_____

because I am human

_____

because I took the wrong posture

_____

because I believe in love

_____

because the in between doesn't matter

_____

Chapter 5

"Some chapters will never have enough pages,
especially if you're only writing for yourself.
You belong to me and I to you. Share!"

KG

Rise

The earth in you is drawn
to the anticline of existence
your feet are planted firm
your legs are sculpted
to dance through torrential rains,
waves from Yemoja,
fountains of fertility
you are both mermaid
and terra steward
so rise with the lantern of the world
see the path illuminated
and concentrate on one step at a time
rise!

Sun Kissed

Melatonin brewed to a simmer
eyes closed like a vault recounting the day
a day with the Sun at its Plymouth, sun-kissing my
forehead
tanned between "black and blue"

I was graced by words to tag my inner ambitions
"What did you dream about?" her voice ricocheting
between my ascent to waking consciousness
I stared up in silence
wrestling with memory, I explored …

not one latent thought available for recall
but I could feel a dream in my bones
erect in my pursuit of self actualization
somehow I found myself excavating a missing artifact

sizing it against empty space
it fit flush along my amygdala
a dream undreamt
I could rationalize this dream without pictures

"what did you dream," she would not deviate from her ask
this time
"I dreamt of you"
the ocean washed away invading thoughts
it was time to swim

Imagined

If you've ever looked beyond the stars
and petitioned the heavens from afar

yearned that the great unknown
would grant you a peace beyond understanding

that it would mute out all inadequacies
commanding them to crash into the sun's gravity

reaffirming a space of purified renewal
on gamma rays under arched rainbows

I assure you that the Angels see your spirit
dancing like royalty
tenacious, resilient, bold
you are beautiful, elegant, strong
a friend so dear

I say to you

here I am
now
and forever
here I am

if you've ever fixed your eyes upon a mirror
and rushed to turn away quickly
because the reflection was so skewed

in elongating detachments

stitched with threads too thick to needle wronged hues
protruding

through smoothed powdered expressions
and jarred confessions preserved in illusions of a WE

I say

brave your heart
to focus on the garden
emerging from your iris of harvesting green

here I am
now
and forever
here I am

if you've ever questioned an intent
in a moment of time doubting it's sustainability

against values filtering away
wasted energy escaping your orbit for conquests
to colonize moons with seas of sand and oceans of dust

I'll remind you still you rise
rooted in fertile reality interlocking beneath
the influences of storms you're built to endure

I say

may my firmness in love be a refuge In times of retreat
and a battering ram in times of war

here I am
now
and forever

here I am

Renovations

Built in 1980 with materials from Glaspie and Lee
a single dwelling and numerous modifications to date
the waste of not recycling the "under construction" sign
it's in perpetual use
this project will surely not be the last

the price tag of me is way over budget
the brisk of winter chill frosting windows
the hearts I draw in glass last but a second
holiday blues
boiler pipes clinging
these old veins trying to disperse steam

I want to invite you in but it's loud and cold
there's dust everywhere
inhabitable without dreaming
intolerable with understanding
in this moment, that is my home
please don't judge my renovations for I borrowed the
wrong designs
under construction

At Least I Showed You

My intent was pure
sincere, potent, real

it was full
clear, honest, rare

I would dare say
selfless, open,
but too soon

perhaps it was laziness
to not search for
better words than

"I love you"

I committed my heart to my mouth
and my mouth to my heart

ran off to a fantasy
where we would never be apart

ignoring hints bubbling through
"Who are you?
acknowledging I exist but holding on to resist

your healing,
your champion,
your advocate,
your muse,
your partner,

your compliment,
your surrender,
yours

how I want you to fall into my arms
and cast all uncertainties upon my shoulders

I was shaped by fire for you

more than words
I heard actioned factions murmuring beneath
precursors of your identity

processing yesterday

you were there, naked
in ownership of regret
that you've bypassed

prerequisites, equating to hesitance
you mourned a gaping hole too fresh
too deep

so I showed you
what love would do

knowing I couldn't get a second back
knowing I would only be preparing you for beyond

I showed you

that every feeling you have
should be respected

acknowledged, honored

that every thought
should be explored
nurtured
embraced
protected

your forever, meant forever
your everything, meant everything
your go, meant going
your stay, staying

dear heart
you can't find what you are
not searching for

and your default
is to anchor down
in their departure
how I want you to know my
love leaves no room

for deceit
wandering eyes
disguised in careers
of romantic reparations

love is patience,
forgiveness,
over and over,
squared over

magnetic poles
sensitive to your internal compass
knee deep in relational compost

a toast
to unleashing all that laid dormant
in your "yes"
you said "no"
to you

so I'm careful not
to deny you a desire
coaching you free

of limitations
repression
of tolerance
I say what is needed
to build a core

matured
to adore
To show you
you are more than deserving of any soul
enrolled in advanced healing

so I'll show you what love would do

knowing I can't get a second back
knowing I would only be preparing you for beyond

I'll show you

for a second
what could be different
I am different

nothing of your past
a springboard to your future
heal here
this is safe

heal there
while I change hats
de-crowning my arrival
to what felt like home

rationalized in superstition
they say it's bad luck
to put fedoras on beds
so I seal up head to toe
diver's gear

there will be caves flooded
no oxygen there
sounds muffled

refractions mirage
I'll focus on corners draped with curtains
peppered with soviet landmines

nothing shall detonate by human error
the terror
facing outward
inward
we are in danger

of miscalculating tomorrow
I swallow shallow graves made hallow

smile your way through
as you are different
there's room to imagine all
that is possible

through manifesting blessings beyond sight
there's no right
nor wrong
just strong
passions and desire
that must live forward

without infringement
the sentiment of trusting
impulse
you'll find a space worth defending
a refuse worth building

and when your not rooted

I'll remind you of what love would do

knowing I can't get a second back
knowing I would only be preparing you for beyond

I'll show you

you are love, loved

I am Not Tripping

Blood stained memories
I embody survival of the fittest
unlike many, I have lived in a third-world country
called Poverty
borders of triple-pained glass
and great walls of class
division
I see differences
contradictions
false depictions
in the distance too far to correct immediately

will, focus, I shape success
prayer, notice, I am not like the rest
for right or wrong
I move forward

on this journey I have packed lite
necessities, recipes
ancestry telepathy
I seek oneness with one food source
rain and it's opposite
dry spells indeed
but hey

I'm not tripping

I have witnessed the expiration of life
abruptly and gradually
cultivation of life naturally and systemically
hate

institutionalized and rationalized

distractions
mobilized in disguise of a want so strong that it resembles a
need
obsession
with that thing that consumes so much of you
that you loose you

in time
in space
relevant to motion
rooted in systems of governing
we trust freedom and lives to an alliance of "free" markets
structured upon an arbitrary substance with limited function
insight to the value we place on external beauty
shallowness consistent throughout

but little do my words matter
for my truest essence lies beneath my surface
but hey

I'm not tripping

I once conformed to the crab in the bucket analogy
by capitalizing off of others addictions, convictions
encrypted in the hippocampus
late to campus
but lessons learnt
I found my resolve
resiliency proven
I am an acquired taste
hate me or love me, there is no in between

there is certainty in me
I will weather the storms

there is certainty in you
for it will not be long
before you are tested
by uncharted places
frames of mind
circumstances beyond your control
momentum from behind
random influences
others be design

Facebook!
Twitter!
auctioned is your time
herded sleepwalkers
but if anyone is awake
It's you
so if they ask me, you know my position

I am not tripping

Masterpiece

I dreamt of her at the summit my highest ambition
the cool of the Mount Sinai chilled my thoughts to a slow

a masterpiece by every stretch of the imagination
brilliance realized through a design so sweet

the winged fruit of a Samara
freckled golden oak wrapped with silk
craving a build with glass steel

her potential like kited balloons
toned and textured evidence of life
beyond here

so I poured love over love
brush in hand
this paint won't dry

When I Go

Before I am placed to rest
and my spirit leaves this body
when my eyes close for good
and this vessel suffers no more

may I look you into your eyes
and acknowledge your worth
marvel in the beauty that is you
without interruptions from faults

YOU ARE LOVED

Made in the USA
Columbia, SC
08 June 2022